BIG-NOTE PIANO
CLASSIC COUNTRY

ISBN 978-1-4584-0843-3

HAL•LEONARD®
CORPORATION

7777 W. BLUEMOUND RD. P.O. BOX 13819 MILWAUKEE, WI 53213

Visit Hal Leonard Online at
www.halleonard.com

ACHY BREAKY HEART
(Don't Tell My Heart)

Words and Music by
DON VON TRESS

You can tell the world you nev-er was my girl.____
You can tell your ma I moved to Ark-an-sas.____

6

ALWAYS ON MY MIND

Words and Music by WAYNE THOMPSON,
MARK JAMES and JOHNNY CHRISTOPHER

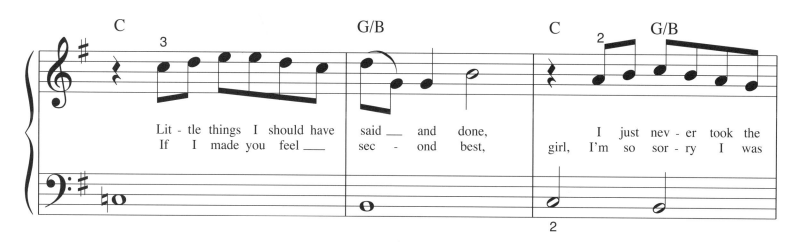

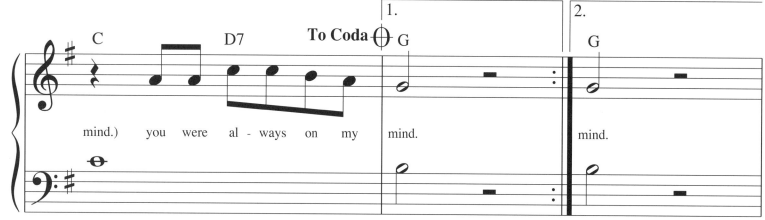

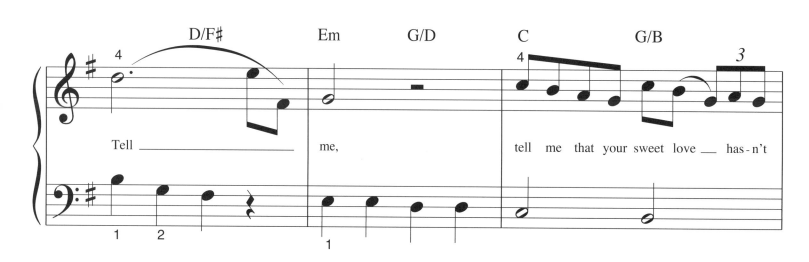

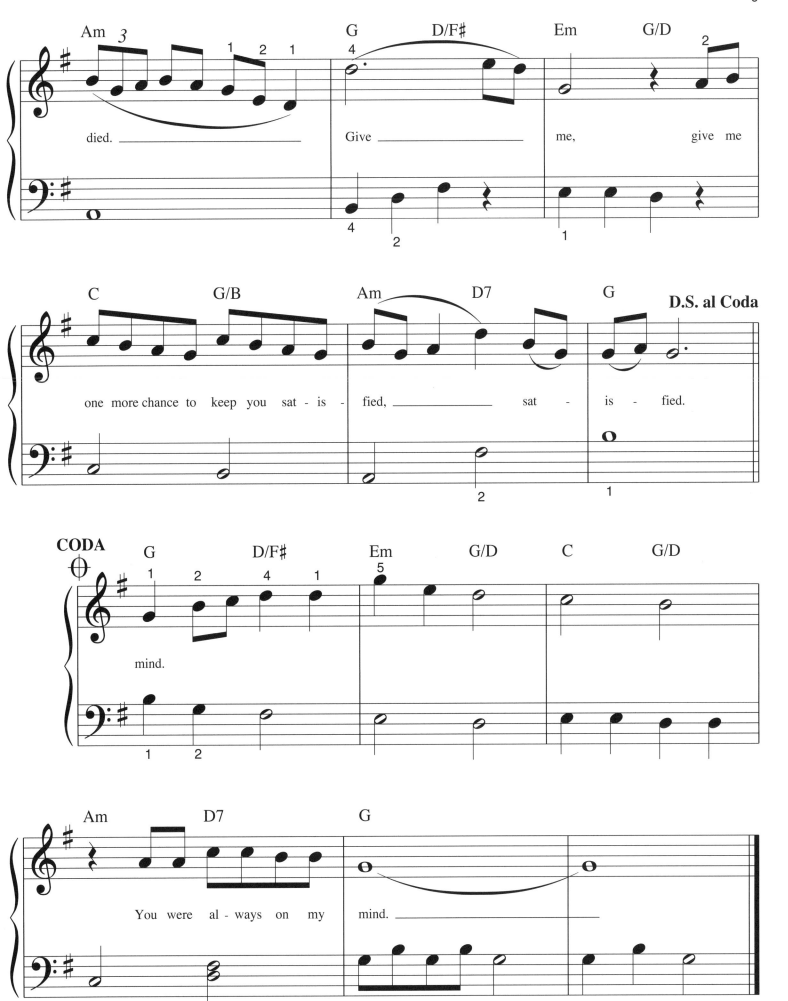

BALLAD OF A TEENAGE QUEEN

Words and Music by
JACK CLEMENT

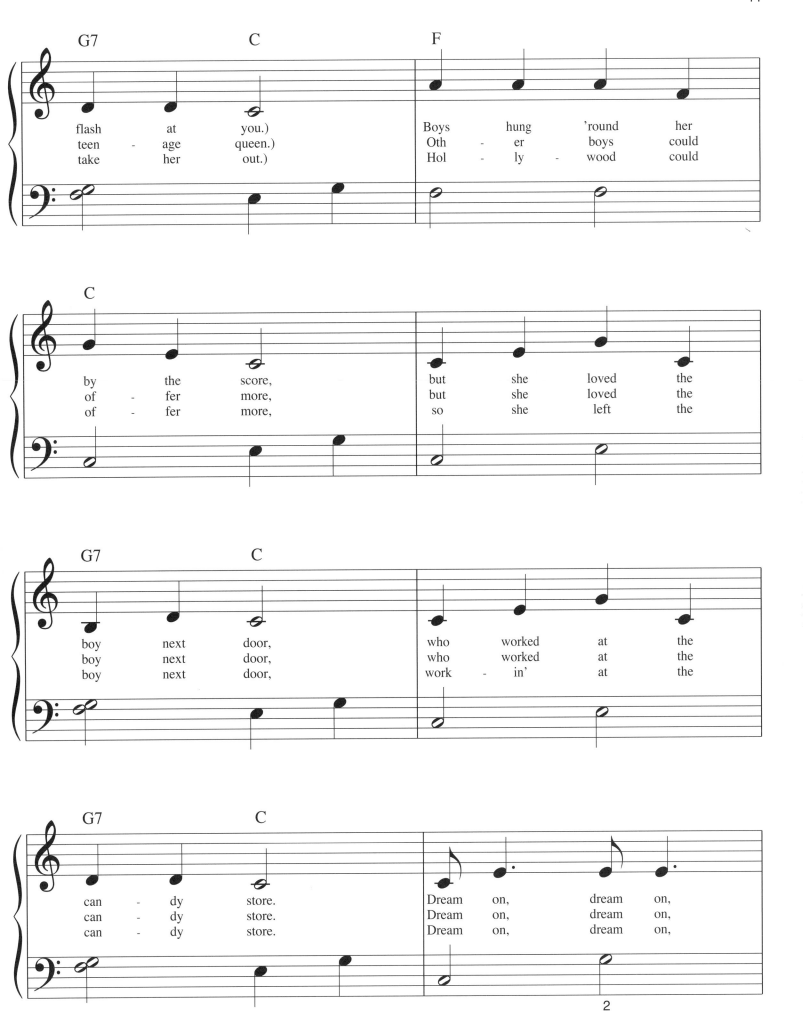

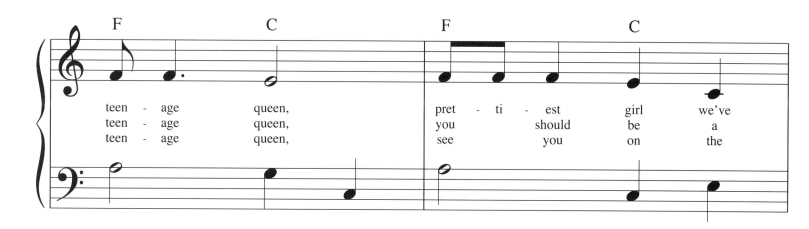

teen - age queen, pret - ti - est girl we've
teen - age queen, you should be a
teen - age queen, see you on the

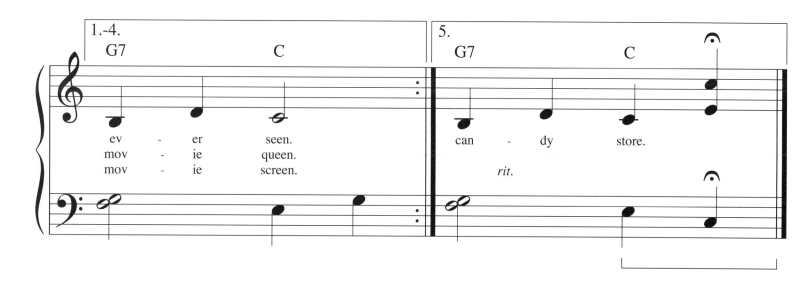

1.-4.
ev - er seen.
mov - ie queen.
mov - ie screen.

5.
can - dy store.

rit.

Additional Lyrics

4. Very soon she was a star, pretty house and shiny cars,
   Swimming pool and a fence around, but she missed her old home town.
   (But she missed her old home town)
   All the world was at her door,
   All except the boy next door, who worked at the candy store.
   Dream on, dream on, teenage queen, saddest girl we've ever seen.

5. Then one day the teenage star sold her house and all her cars.
   Gave up all her wealth and fame, left it all and caught a train.
   (Left it all and caught a train)
   Do I have to tell you more?
   She came back to the boy next door, who worked at the candy store.
   Now this story has some more; you'll hear it all at the candy store.

BOOT SCOOTIN' BOOGIE

Words and Music by
RONNIE DUNN

CRAZY

Words and Music by
WILLIE NELSON

FOR THE GOOD TIMES

Words and Music by
KRIS KRISTOFFERSON

FOLSOM PRISON BLUES

Words and Music by
JOHN R. CASH

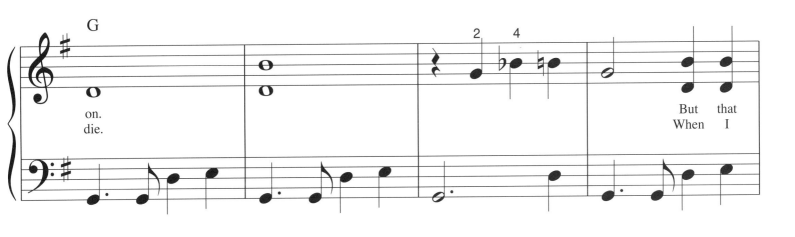

Additional Lyrics

3. I bet there's rich folks eatin' in a fancy dining car.
   They're prob'ly drinkin' coffee and smokin' big cigars,
   But I know I had it comin', I know I can't be free,
   But those people keep a-movin', and that's what tortures me.

4. Well, if they freed me from this prison, if that railroad train was mine,
   I bet I'd move on over a little farther down the line,
   Far from Folsom Prison, that's where I want to stay,
   And I'd let that lonesome whistle blow my blues away.

GEORGIA ON MY MIND

Words by STUART GORRELL
Music by HOAGY CARMICHAEL

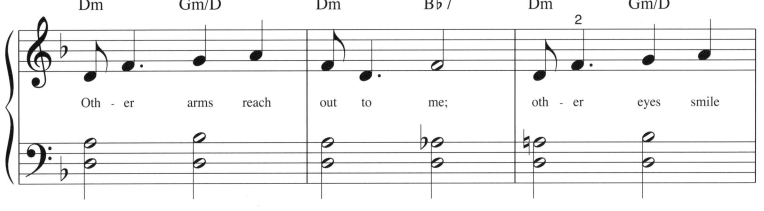

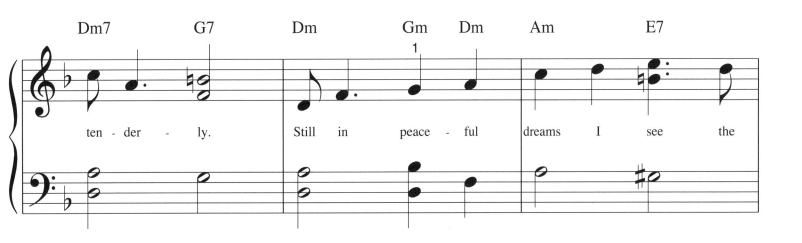

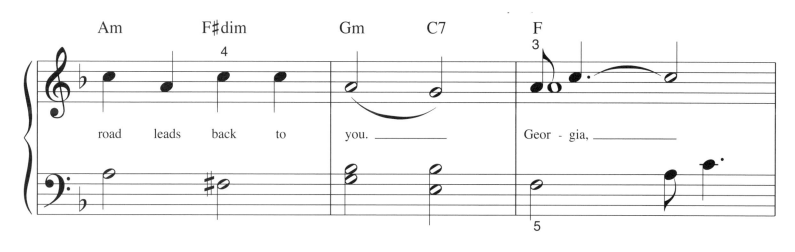

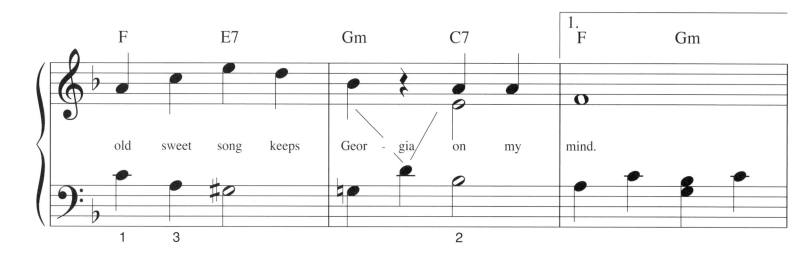

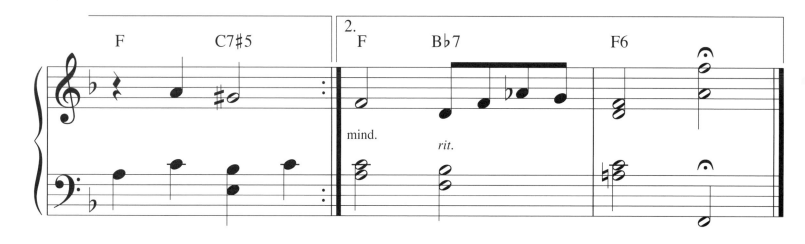

HE STOPPED LOVING HER TODAY

Words and Music by BOBBY BRADDOCK
and CURLY PUTMAN

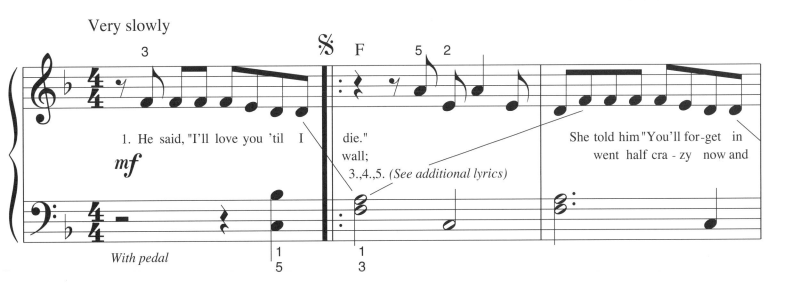

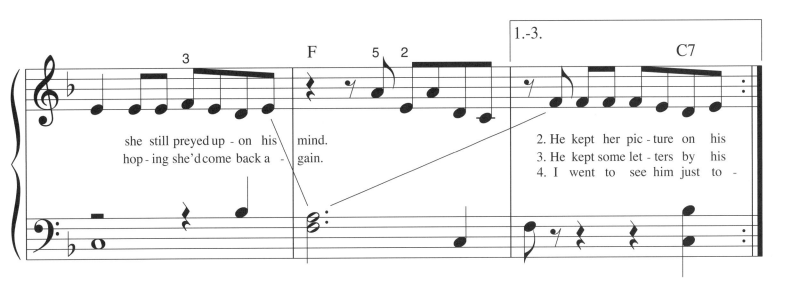

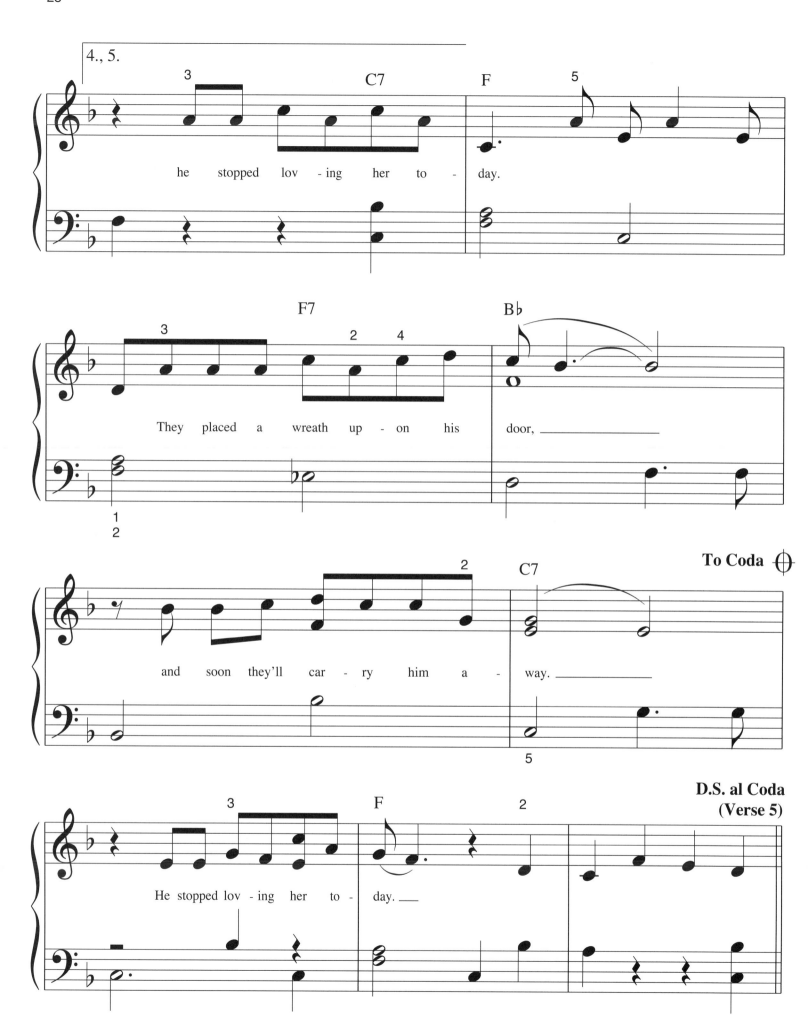

CODA

He stopped lov - ing her to - day. _____

Additional Lyrics

3. He kept some letters by his bed, dated 1962.
   He had underlined in red every single, "I love you."

4. I went to see him just today, oh, but I didn't see no tears:
   All dressed up to go away, first time I'd seen him smile in years.
   Chorus

5. *(Spoken)* You know, she came to see him one last time.
   We all wondered if she would.
   And it came running through my mind,
   This time he's over her for good.
   Chorus

GREEN GREEN GRASS OF HOME

Words and Music by
CURLY PUTMAN

Gentle shuffle

HEARTACHES BY THE NUMBER

Words and Music by
HARLAN HOWARD

Two step

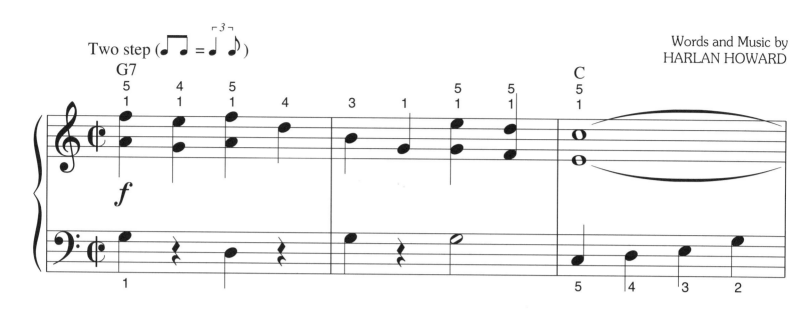

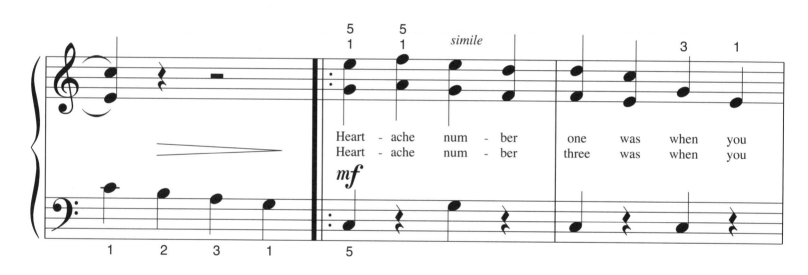

Heart - ache num - ber one was when you
Heart - ache num - ber three was when you

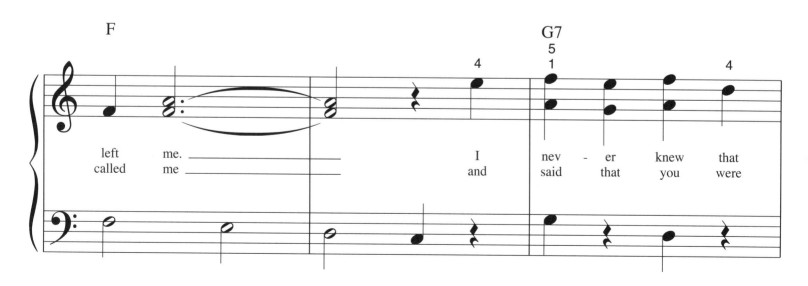

left me.
called me

I
and

nev - er knew that
said that you were

day   that   I   stop   count - ing,   that's   the

day   my   world   will   end.

day   my   world   will   end.

cresc.

HEARTBREAK HOTEL

Words and Music by MAE BOREN AXTON,
TOMMY DURDEN and ELVIS PRESLEY

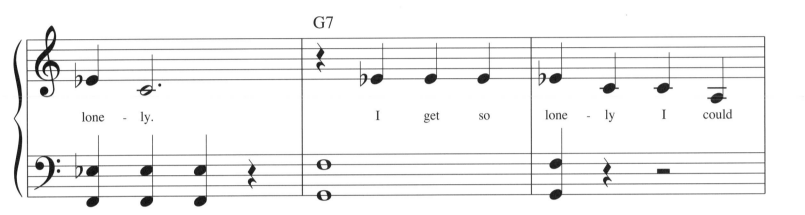

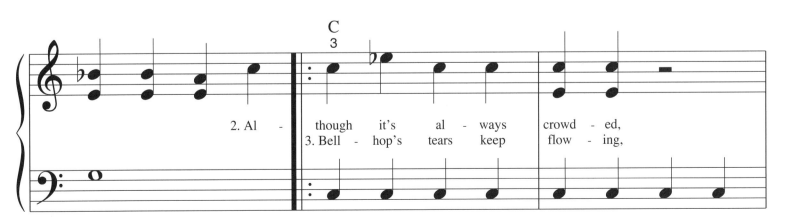

still can find ___ some room, where those bro - ken -
desk clerks dressed _ in black. They been so

heart - ed lov - ers cry a - way their gloom, oh! I get so
long on Lone - ly Street they ain't nev- er gon' come back, oh!

F7

lone - ly, I get so lone - ly, get so

G7

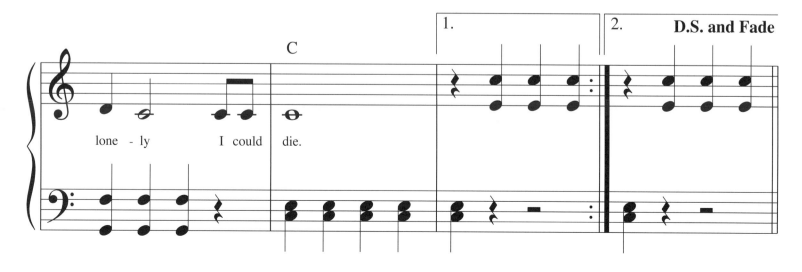

lone - ly I could die.

C

1.

2. **D.S. and Fade**

KING OF THE ROAD

Words and Music by
ROGER MILLER

Moderate shuffle

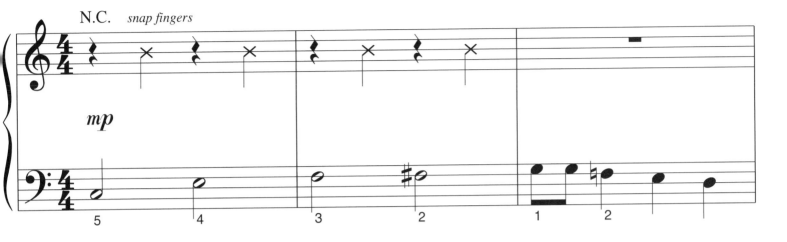

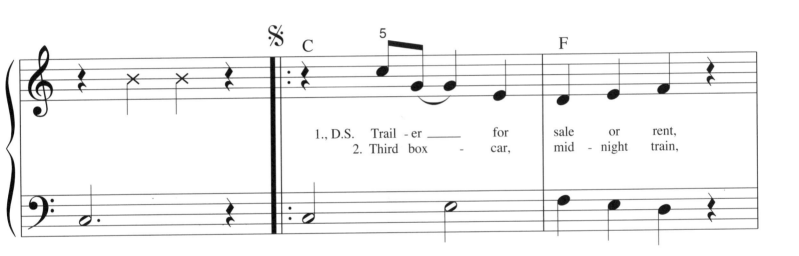

1., D.S. Trail - er _____ for sale or rent,
2. Third box - car, mid - night train,

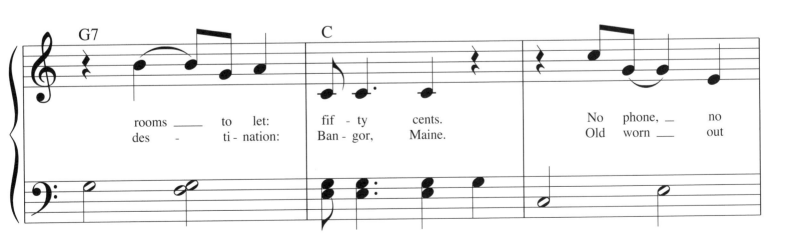

rooms _____ to let: fif - ty cents.
des - ti - nation: Ban - gor, Maine.

No phone, __ no
Old worn __ out

HELP ME MAKE IT
THROUGH THE NIGHT

Words and Music by
KRIS KRISTOFFERSON

Moderately

Take the rib - bon from your hair, side
Come and lay down by my gone
Yes - ter - day is dead and

Shake it loose and let it
Till the ear - ly morn - in'
And to - mor - row's out of

44

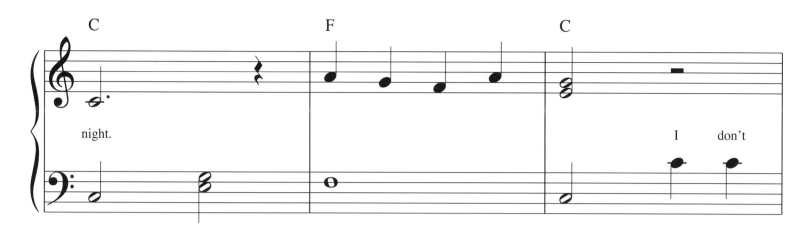

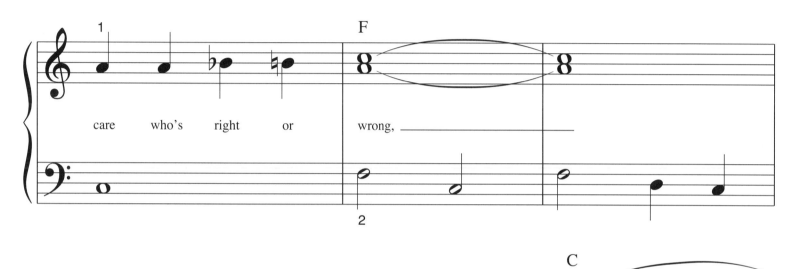

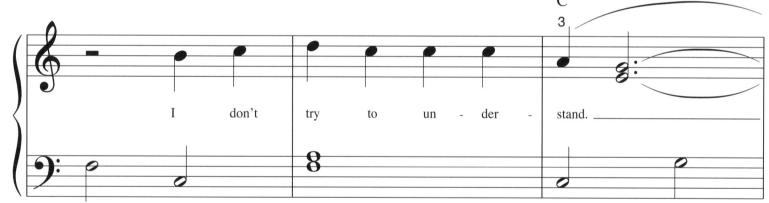

HERE YOU COME AGAIN

Words by CYNTHIA WEIL
Music by BARRY MANN

Here you come a - gain. ____
Here you come a - gain. ____

Just when I've ____ be - gun to get my - self to - geth - er, you
Just when I'm ____ a - bout to make it work with - out you, you

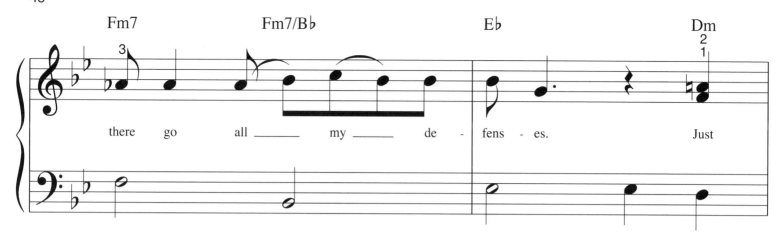

there go all _____ my _____ de - fens - es. Just

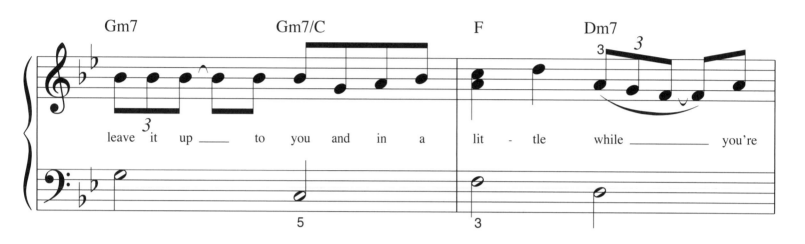

leave it up _____ to you and in a lit - tle while _____ you're

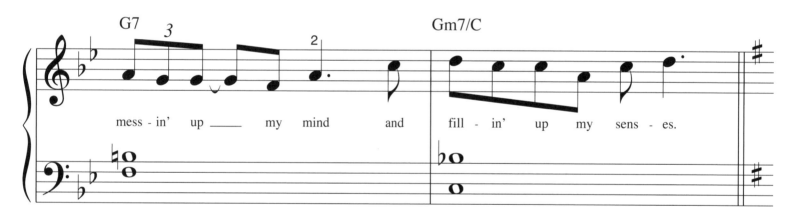

mess - in' up _____ my mind and fill - in' up my sens - es.

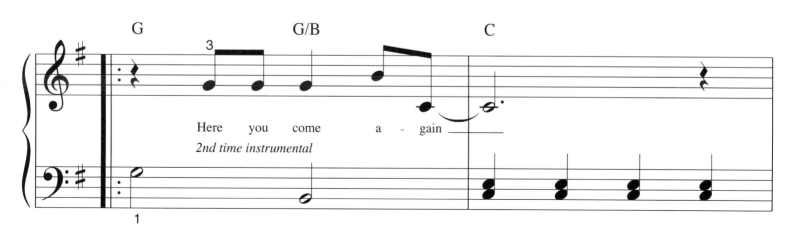

Here you come a - gain _____

2nd time instrumental

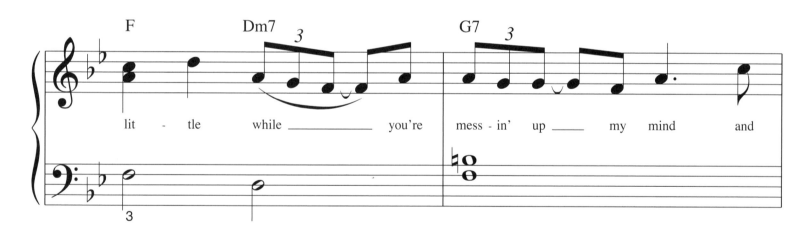

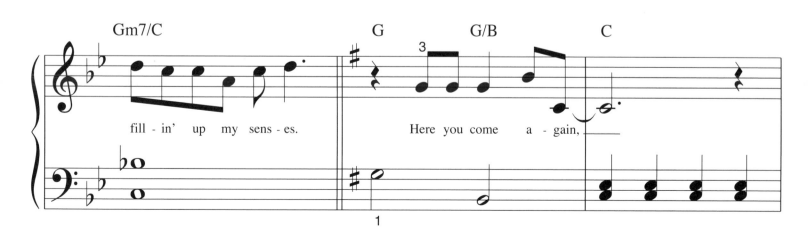

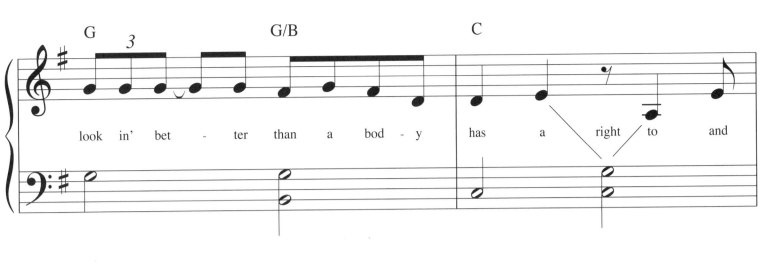

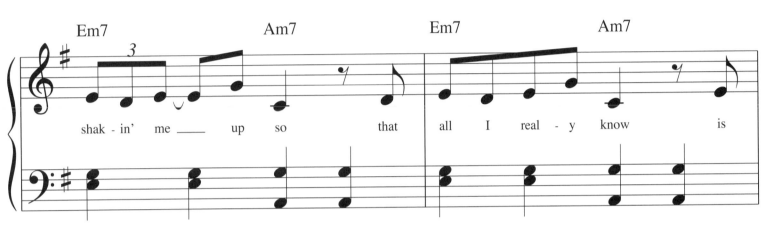

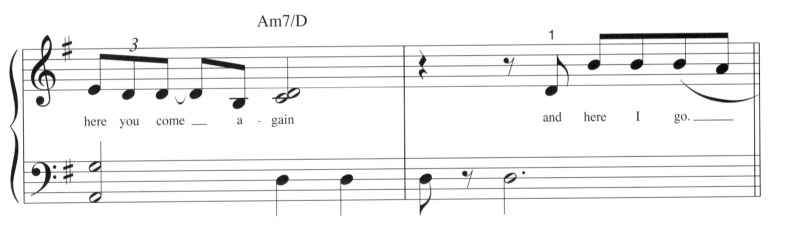

Repeat and Fade

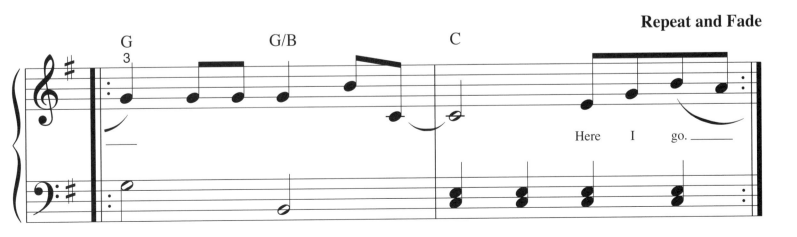

I FALL TO PIECES

Words and Music by HANK COCHRAN
and HARLAN HOWARD

I WALK THE LINE

Words and Music by
JOHN R. CASH

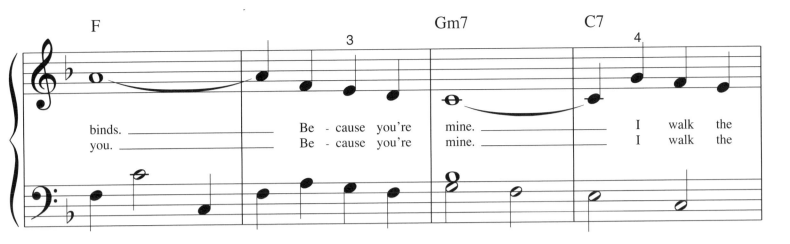

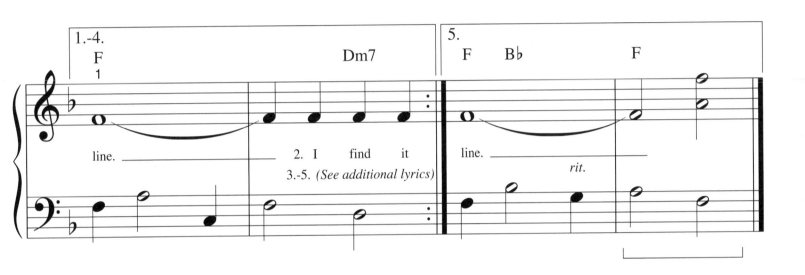

Additional Lyrics

3. As sure as night is dark and day is light,
   I keep you on my mind both day and night.
   And happiness I've known proves that it's right.
   Because you're mine I walk the line.

4. You've got a way to keep me on your side.
   You give me cause for love that I can't hide.
   For you I know I'd even try to turn the tide.
   Because you're mine I walk the line.

5. I keep a close watch on this heart of mine.
   I keep my eyes wide open all the time.
   I keep the ends out for the tie that binds.
   Because you're mine I walk the line.

MAKE THE WORLD GO AWAY

Words and Music by
HANK COCHRAN

MAMMAS DON'T LET YOUR BABIES GROW UP TO BE COWBOYS

Words and Music by ED BRUCE
and PATSY BRUCE

60

He's If you can't un - der - stand him and
He's not wrong, he's just dif - f'rent and

he don't die
his pride won't

young, He'll
let him do

prob - a - bly
things to make

just ride _____ a - way.
you think _____ he's right.

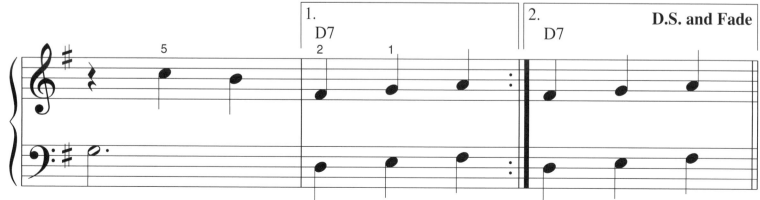

1.
D7

2.
D7

D.S. and Fade

WHAT'S FOREVER FOR

Words and Music by
RAFE VAN HOY

SMOKY MOUNTAIN RAIN

Words and Music by KYE FLEMING
and DENNIS MORGAN

Smok- y Moun - tain rain, ____ I'll keep on

search - ing; I can't go on hurt - ing this way. ____ She's

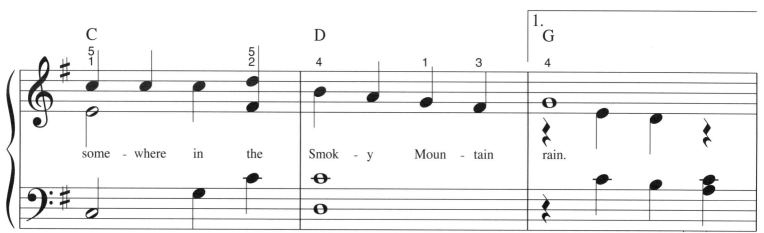

some - where in the Smok - y Moun - tain rain.

TO ALL THE GIRLS I'VE LOVED BEFORE

Lyric by HAL DAVID
Music by ALBERT HAMMOND

72

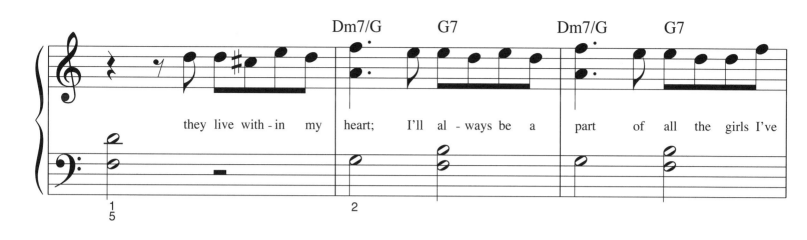

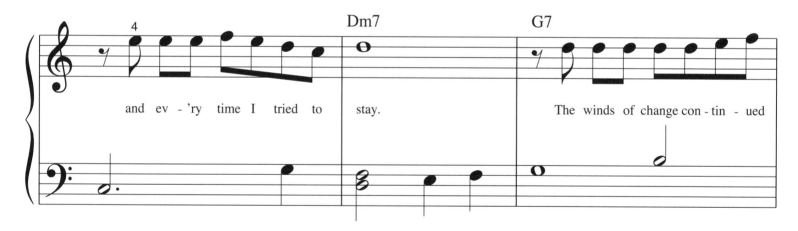

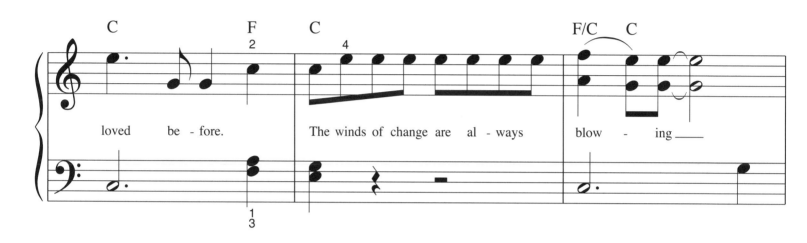

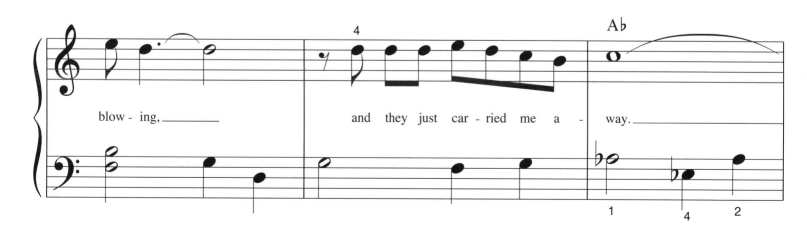

YOU ARE MY SUNSHINE

Words and Music by
JIMMIE DAVIS

75

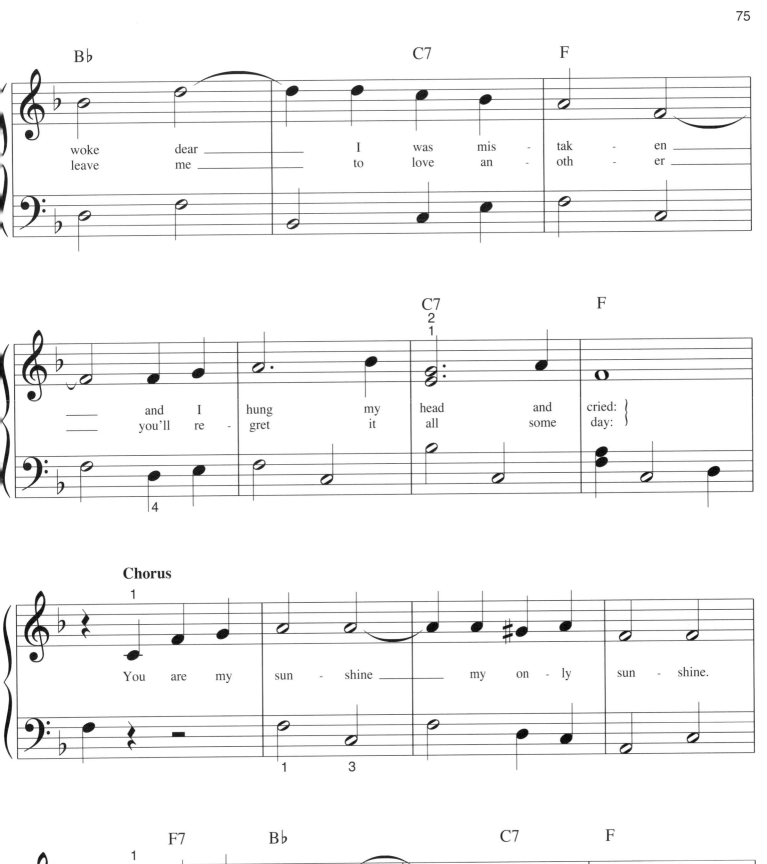

Additional Lyrics

3. You told me once dear you really loved me
   And no one else could come between.
   But now you've left me and love another
   You have shattered all my dreams:
   Chorus

YOUR CHEATIN' HEART

Words and Music by
HANK WILLIAMS

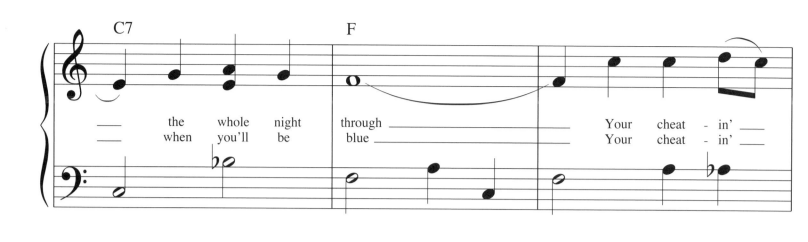

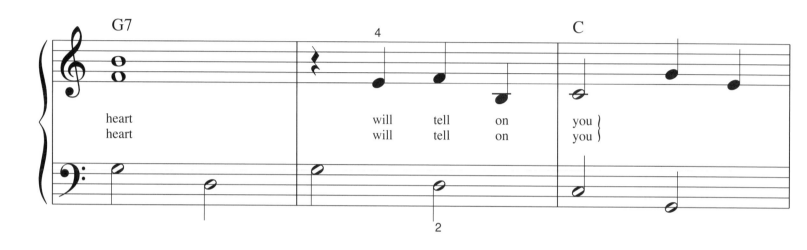

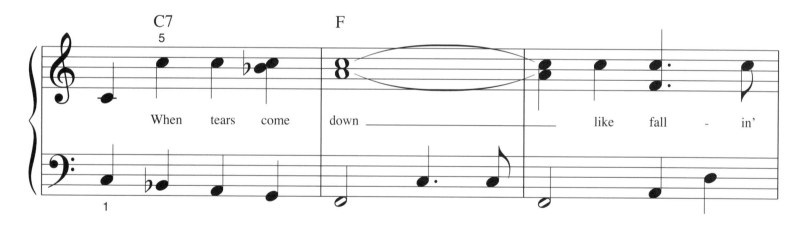

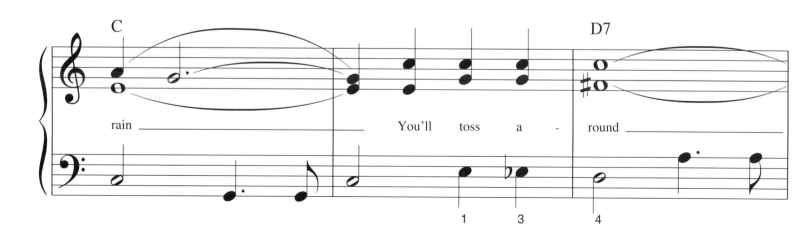

BIG FUN WITH BIG-NOTE PIANO BOOKS!
These songbooks feature exciting easy arrangements for beginning piano students.

Beatles' Best
27 classics for beginners to enjoy, including: Can't Buy Me Love • Eleanor Rigby • Hey Jude • Michelle • Here, There and Everywhere • When I'm Sixty-Four • Yesterday • and more.
00222561 ....$10.95

The Best Songs Ever
70 favorites, featuring: Body and Soul • Crazy • Edelweiss • Fly Me to the Moon • Georgia on My Mind • Imagine • The Lady Is a Tramp • Memory • A String of Pearls • Tears in Heaven • Unforgettable • You Are So Beautiful • and more.
00310425 ....$19.95

Children's Favorite Movie Songs
arranged by Phillip Keveren
16 favorites from films, including: The Bare Necessities • Beauty and the Beast • Can You Feel the Love Tonight • Do-Re-Mi • The Rainbow Connection • Tomorrow • Zip-A-Dee-Doo-Dah • and more.
00310838 ....$10.95

Classical Music's Greatest Hits
24 beloved classical pieces, including: Air on the G String • Ave Maria • By the Beautiful Blue Danube • Canon in D • Eine Kleine Nachtmusik • Für Elise • Ode to Joy • Romeo and Juliet • Waltz of the Flowers • more.
00310475 ....$9.95

Country Hits for Big-Note Piano
14 country classics: Amazed • Bless the Broken Road • Blue • Breathe • Concrete Angel • I Hope You Dance • Jesus Take the Wheel • You're Still the One • and more.
00311815 ....$10.95

Disney Big-Note Collection
Over 40 Disney favorites, including: Circle of Life • Colors of the Wind • Hakuna Matata • It's a Small World • Under the Sea • A Whole New World • Winnie the Pooh • Zip-A-Dee-Doo-Dah • and more.
00316056 ....$19.95

Essential Classical
22 simplified piano pieces from top composers, including: Ave Maria (Schubert) • Blue Danube Waltz (Strauss) • Für Elise (Beethoven) • Jesu, Joy of Man's Desiring (Bach) • Morning (Grieg) • Pomp and Circumstance (Elgar) • and many more.
00311205 ....$9.95

Elton John – Greatest Hits
16 of his biggest hits, including: Bennie and the Jets • Candle in the Wind • Crocodile Rock • Rocket Man • Sacrifice • Your Song • and more.
00221832 ....$10.95

Favorite Children's Songs
arranged by Bill Boyd
29 easy arrangements of songs to play and sing with children: Peter Cottontail • I Whistle a Happy Tune • It's a Small World • On the Good Ship Lollipop • The Rainbow Connection • and more!
00240251 ....$10.95

Hannah Montana
SONGS FROM AND INSPIRED BY THE HIT TV SERIES
13 songs from the hit Disney Channel show: The Best of Both Worlds • I Got Nerve • If We Were a Movie • Pop Princess • Who Said • more!
00316120 ....$14.95

High School Musical 3
11 songs: The Boys Are Back • Can I Have This Dance • High School Musical • I Want It All • Just Wanna Be with You • A Night to Remember • Now or Never • Right Here Right Now • Scream • Walk Away • We're All in This Together (Graduation Version).
00316127 ....$14.99

Movie Hits
20 songs popularized on the silver screen, including: Breakaway • I Believe I Can Fly • I Will Remember You • Kokomo • Somewhere Out There • Tears in Heaven • What a Wonderful World • and more.
00221804 ....$10.95

The Phantom of the Opera
9 songs from the Broadway spectacular, including: All I Ask of You • Angel of Music • Masquerade • The Music of the Night • The Phantom of the Opera • The Point of No Return • Prima Donna • Think of Me • Wishing You Were Somehow Here Again.
00110006 ....$12.95

Pride & Prejudice
MUSIC FROM THE MOTION PICTURE SOUNDTRACK
12 piano pieces from the 2006 Oscar-nominated film: Another Dance • Darcy's Letter • Georgiana • Leaving Netherfield • Liz on Top of the World • Meryton Townhall • The Secret Life of Daydreams • Stars and Butterflies • and more.
00316125 ....$10.95

The Sound of Music
arranged by Phillip Keveren
9 favorites: Climb Ev'ry Mountain • Do-Re-Mi • Edelweiss • The Lonely Goatherd • Maria • My Favorite Things • Sixteen Going on Seventeen • So Long, Farewell • The Sound of Music.
00316057 ....$10.95

Today's Pop Hits
14 of today's hottest hits: Beautiful • Clocks • Complicated • Don't Know Why • Drift Away • Fallen • Heaven • A Moment Like This • 100 Years • Pieces of Me • She Will Be Loved • A Thousand Miles • You Don't Know My Name • You Raise Me Up.
00221817 ....$12.95

Worship Favorites
20 powerful songs: Above All • Come, Now Is the Time to Worship • I Could Sing of Your Love Forever • More Precious Than Silver • Open the Eyes of My Heart • Shout to the Lord • and more.
00311207 ....$10.95

FOR MORE INFORMATION, SEE YOUR LOCAL MUSIC DEALER, OR WRITE TO:

HAL•LEONARD® CORPORATION
7777 W. BLUEMOUND RD. P.O. BOX 13819 MILWAUKEE, WI 53213

Complete song lists online at
www.halleonard.com

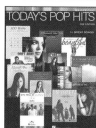